DEC 3 0 2002

Lemurs

by Helen Frost

Ring-tailed lemurs

Consulting Editor: Gail Saunders-Smith, Ph.D.

Consultant: Dorothy Clark
Duke University Primate Center

Pebble Books

an imprint of Capstone Press
Mankato, Minnesota

Pebble Books are published by Capstone Press
151 Good Counsel Drive, P.O. Box 669, Mankato, Minnesota 56002
http://www.capstone-press.com

1 2 3 4 5 6 07 06 05 04 03 02

Library of Congress Cataloging-in-Publication Data
Frost, Helen, 1949–
    Lemurs / by Helen Frost.
        p. cm.—(Rain forest animals)
    Summary: Simple text and photographs present the features and behavior of
lemurs.
    Includes bibliographical references (p. 23) and index.
    ISBN 0-7368-1456-6 (hardcover)
    1. Lemur (Genus)–Juvenile literature. [1. Lemurs. 2. Rain forest animals.]
I. Title.
QL737.P95 F76 2003
599.8'3–dc21   2002001229

Note to Parents and Teachers

The Rain Forest Animals series supports national science standards
related to life science. This book describes and illustrates lemurs
that live in tropical rain forests. The photographs support early
readers in understanding the text. The repetition of words and
phrases helps early readers learn new words. This book also
introduces early readers to subject-specific vocabulary words, which
are defined in the Words to Know section. Early readers may need
assistance to read some words and to use the Table of Contents,
Words to Know, Read More, Internet Sites, and Index/Word List
sections of the book.

Table of Contents

4

Lemurs are small,
furry primates.

Mouse lemur

Lemurs have big eyes.
They have long legs
and a long tail.

Red rutted lemur

places lemurs live

Most lemurs live on the island of Madagascar. Some lemurs live in tropical rain forests on that island.

emergent layer

canopy layer

understory layer

forest floor

10

Lemurs leap from trees in the understory layer and the canopy layer. Some lemurs travel along the forest floor.

Some lemurs travel in groups. Other lemurs travel alone.

Crowned lemurs

Lemurs eat fruit, leaves, and flowers. Some lemurs also eat insects and other small animals.

Sanford's lemur

Lemurs have a good
sense of smell.
Some male lemurs
wave their smelly tails
to scare their rivals.

Ring-tailed lemur

Most lemurs are active during the day. Other kinds of lemurs are active at night.

Red-fronted lemur

Lemurs sleep on branches or in nests.

Ring-tailed lemur

Words to Know

canopy—the layer of treetops that forms a covering over a forest

forest floor—the bottom layer of a forest; almost no sunlight reaches the forest floor.

furry—having soft, thick hair; lemurs' fur can be shades of brown, red, gold, or black.

lemur—a primate that is related to monkeys and apes; there are more than 30 kinds of lemurs.

male—an animal that can father young

primate—any animal in a group that includes humans, apes, and monkeys; primates use their four fingers and one thumb to hold objects.

rival—someone with whom you compete; male lemurs compete with each other during mating season.

tropical rain forest—a thick area of trees where rain falls almost every day; some lemurs live in tropical rain forests.

understory—the lowest layer of trees in a forest

Read More

Butz, Christopher. *Lemurs.* Animals of the Rain Forest. Austin, Texas: Raintree Steck-Vaughn, 2002.

Darling, Kathy. *Lemurs.* On Location. New York: Lothrop, Lee & Shepard, 1998.

Kite, Lorien. *Lemurs.* Nature's Children. Danbury, Conn.: Grolier Educational, 1999.

McDonald, Mary Ann. *Lemurs.* Chanhassen, Minn.: Child's World, 1999.

Internet Sites

Animal Bytes: Lemur
http://www.seaworld.org/AnimalBytes/lemurab.html

Black and White Ruffed Lemur
http://www.scz.org/animals/l/bwlemur.html

Duke University Primate Center
http://www.duke.edu/web/primate

Mammals of the San Antonio Zoo: Lemurs
http://www.sazoo-aq.org/02meet/02sublinks/lemur.html

Index/Word List

Word Count: 118
Early-Intervention Level: 13

Editorial Credits

Martha E. H. Rustad, editor; Linda Clavel and Heidi Meyer, cover designers; Jennifer Schonborn, interior illustrator; Angi Gahler, book designer; Wanda Winch, photo researcher; Karen Risch, product planning editor

Photo Credits

Digital Vision, 8, 20
Erwin and Peggy Bauer, 4
Lynn M. Stone, 16
PhotoDisc, Inc., 1
Sylvia Stevens, 18
Thomas C. Boyden, 14
Tom and Pat Leeson, 6, 12
William Muñoz, cover

The author thanks the children's section staff at the Allen County Public Library in Fort Wayne, Indiana, for research assistance.